FLOODS
ON DRY GROUND

DEDICATION

To my faithful and loving husband who has encouraged me many times to do the things I didn't think I could do.

And to my Jesus, Who brought me into His Kingdom through the Jesus Movement revival. For this reason, I too, "can never be content with anything less than with what I have seen and I live to see it again."

Copyright 2004 by Jessica Meldrum
ISBN 0-9715470-3-3
Library of Congress Catalog Card Number:
TX 6-007-109

Second Edition Printed 2005

Third Edition Printed 2018
Copyright 2018 by Jessica Meldrum
ISBN-13: 978-1985134607
ISBN-10: 1985134608

Printed in the United States of America

In His Presence
Ministries

www.ihpministry.com

CONTENTS

INTRODUCTION

In an obscure part of the world more than 50 years ago God stepped down from heaven and altered eternity. This book was written to share the truth about this revival and what constitutes genuine revival. Many believers are aware that what we call revival or a spiritual awakening in our Western culture falls severely short of the holy visitations that have been recorded in the chronicles of church history. There are others, never having known anything outside of their mediocre faith, doubt that such events portrayed in this book could possibly have happened. In either case, my prayer is that some simple believers will be challenged by the accounts of the Hebrides Awakening and will covenant with God to give Him no rest until He "pours water on the thirsty and floods on dry ground."

Most of the accounts and quotes have been taken from 17 audio tapes of Duncan Campbell or other eyewitnesses. Other resources I've selected for use are from credible historians, two of which were close friends with Duncan Campbell. All materials used are listed in the bibliography.

Revivals are not preceded by the Church becoming
aware of the need, but by a few people here and there,
who, feeling the need, begin to entreat God for a
revival. This sense of need grows into a burden,
until the cry becomes an agony.
This is the cry which God cannot deny.
— James Burns

Of what infinite importance is the place the
intercessor holds in the kingdom of God! Is it not
indeed a matter of wonder that God would give men
such power? Yet there are so few who know
what it is to take hold of His strength
and pray down His blessing on the world.
— Andrew Murray

Our whole being must be in our praying; like John
Knox, we must say and feel, "Give me Scotland, or I
die." We cannot quit praying, because heart and soul
are in our prayers. We pray with all perseverance; we
hang on to our prayers because we live by them,
we press our pleas because we must have them or die.
— E.M . Bounds

Will you not revive us again, that your people
may rejoice in You?
Surely His salvation is near to those who fear Him
That glory may dwell in our land.
Psalm 85:6, 9

chapter one

THE REVIVAL

When God stepped down from heaven in 1949 the things of earth took second place. "An awareness of God was felt everywhere. You felt His presence and His power on meadow and moorland. You met Him in the homes of people. Indeed God was everywhere, you could not escape Him."

Conviction was so intense that people could not sleep, normal activities were halted and lost men and women cried out to God, terrified to face Him in their sins. Strong seamen could be found weeping behind their fishing boats crying out, "God, have mercy on me, a sinner!"

So many young people were converted that the places of entertainment were closed due to lack of interest. "There was no quenching of our desire for the Lord and for the things of God. There was no need to entertain us or put on any special program at the church. We were just hungry for the Word of God itself."

This is revival. It is a supernatural moving of God's Spirit so that "the community suddenly becomes conscious of the moving of God, beginning amongst His own people." Those who previously had no interest in the things of the Lord are suddenly gripped with a divine terror. They plead to God for mercy. Their only thought is to find relief for their souls.

Historically, revival always begins with His people. God's desire is to make His glory known to the church with the ultimate objective of revealing Himself to those who will otherwise face Him in judgment. He wants to heal the land (2 Chr. 7:14), but waits for His people to do their part.

This was a truth that the praying saints understood living on the Isle of Lewis, one in the group of islands making up the Scottish Hebrides (pronounced hĕb´rĭ-dēz´). Thus, in unyielding resolve, they covenanted with their God that they would prepare the way for Him to make known His manifest presence in their community. In response, God brought one of the greatest revivals Scotland has ever seen beginning with the "first wave" from 1949 to 1952.

In the late 1940's, the ministers of the area met to discuss the low spiritual conditions of their churches and "what must be the end should there be no repentance." Together, they composed a resolution to be read on a certain Sunday in all the churches. It called on believers to "view with concern the barrenness of the parishes" so that they would "turn again unto the Lord whom we have so grieved with our waywardness and iniquities." It also implored the people to pray that the communities be "visited with a spirit of repentance."

Many of the believers in the Hebrides immediately went to their knees, petitioning God to visit the islands as He had done in 1939. The Lord had brought in a great harvest through this powerful, layman's revival. Those who experienced the '39 outpouring knew what they were looking for and understood the cost.

John Murdo Smith recalled, "There were watchmen on the walls of Zion who resorted to prayer and would not accept things as they were. Prayer meetings for revival were held in various Christian homes. . . . Those who engaged in prayer and believed God would answer, continued to pray until the power of God came."[i]

Two such prayer warriors were Peggy and Christine Smith of Barvas on Lewis Island. They were 82 and 84 years of age, one blind and the other arthritic. Their poor health did not allow them to be in church as often as they liked but their home was a sanctuary, a place where they daily met with God in prayer.

Peggy and Christine were much concerned about the absence of young people in their church. Their pastor, Reverend James Murray MacKay had tried many things to bring the young people in, but was unsuccessful. Therefore, the Smith sisters willingly chose to pay the price and gave themselves to days and nights of prayer. They constantly reminded the Lord of His promise to "pour water on the thirsty and floods on dry ground (Isa. 44:3)."

One night Peggy received a vision from the Lord. In it she saw her church filled with young people and a man she had never seen before in the pulpit. The next day she sent for her pastor. Having told Reverend MacKay the vision, the minister asked Peggy what should be done. She suggested "Try two nights a week of waiting on God." She advised him to gather some men together to pray on Tuesday and Friday nights from 10:00 in the evening until 4:00 in the morning. She and Christine would do the same in their cottage as their health allowed. The minister agreed and found seven men willing to meet two nights a week in a barn to wait on God until revival came.

For months the two little prayer groups of Barvas prayed on, reminding God of His promise to pour water on dry ground. Early one morning in the barn a young man, Kenneth MacDonald, challenged the others by reading from Psalms 24. "Who shall ascend into the hill of the Lord? Or who shall stand in his holy place? He that hath clean hands, and a pure heart . . . he shall receive the blessing from the Lord."

Addressing the men he declared, "It seems to me [a waste of time] to be praying as we are praying, to be waiting as we are waiting, if we ourselves are not rightly related to God.

"Brethren," Kenneth said, "We have been praying for months for revival, pleading before God, but I want to ask you a question. Are your hands clean? Are your hearts pure?" The young man then fell on his knees, lifted his hands and cried "God are my hands clean? Is my heart pure?" In response to this penetrating challenge, they fell on their knees in confession and repentance. At that moment the Holy Spirit was unleashed. His glory swept into the barn causing several to fall to the ground under the power of God. Revival had at last come! These men later acknowledged that this experience revealed to them the truth that when the Lord comes He always comes as a *Holy* God. There is an unalterable link between holiness and revival.

One minister recounting this event said, "When that happened in the barn a power was let loose in Barvas that shook the whole of Lewis. God stepped down. The Holy Spirit began to move among the people. God seemed to be everywhere. An awareness of God gripped the whole community. So much so that work stopped. Men would meet in a field and begin to talk about God in the midst."

Pastor Mackay testified, "You felt His presence and His power on meadow and moorland. Indeed, God was everywhere, you could not escape Him." This was revival. Not a new program, not a new teaching, not an evangelistic effort, nor anything contrived by man.

In view of what was happening an evangelist, Duncan Campbell, was sent for by Pastor MacKay. The invitation was at first turned down due to a scheduling problem. However, Peggy Smith stood firm. Certain that it was Mr. Campbell she had seen in her vision; she told the minister that this was "what man is saying. He will be here in 10 days." And so he was, God intervened, canceling the convention Campbell was to speak at.

The minister and an elder met him at a local pier. The first question put to Campbell by the elder was, "Mr. Campbell, I would like to ask you a question before you leave the pier. Are you walking with God?" To which he replied, "I think I can say this, I fear God."

Campbell submitted his first report to the Faith Mission from Barvas on December 14, 1949. "I began my mission on Wednesday night in the parish church. People gathered from all over the parish and we had a congregation of over 300. The meeting began at 7:00 and ended at 10:45 pm. I preached twice during the evening. This was repeated on Thursday and Friday. Yesterday I preached in three different churches to crowded meetings. At the last meeting the Lord manifested His power in a gracious way, and the cry of the anxious was heard all over the church. I closed the service but the people would not go away, so I gathered the anxious ones beneath the pulpit and, along with the minister did what we could to lead them to Christ."[ii]

News spread over the island of what was taking place in Barvas and soon busloads of people were coming from several villages. God began to move in churches and in many house meetings on Lewis. Work and normal activities were set aside for people to get right with God and for Christians to seek out those who had not yet met the Savior.

"The awful presence of God brought a wave of conviction of sin that caused even mature Christians to feel their sinfulness, bringing groans of distress and prayers of repentance from the unconverted. Strong men were bowed under the weight of sin and cries for mercy mingled with shouts of joy from others who had passed into life."[iii]

One night, "young people were at a dance in the parish hall. They weren't thinking of God or eternity. God was not in their thoughts. They were there to have a good night when suddenly, the power of God fell upon the dance. In a matter of minutes the hall was empty. They fled from the hall as a man fleeing from the plague and they made for the church." This is what Peggy had seen in her vision; God's house full of young people.

For the next three years Duncan Campbell's days and nights were filled with meetings in many different parishes. At times, he was asked to speak at a village he had not yet been to and all he could tell them was that he would be there but not until 1:00 am. When he finally arrived, the church would be full.

Many of the ministers on the Isle of Lewis were overwhelmed with the demands to hold services or prayer meetings at all hours of the day and night. The house meetings were filled to suffocation. Numerous conversions took place in homes such as the Morrison cottage in Shader. On December 11th several were converted in this home where the people spontaneously gathered after an earlier church service conducted by Campbell and MacKay.

The presence of God filled Lewis and eventually other islands. His presence "was so powerful that you were constantly living in the expectation that something was about to happen. You would feel a sort of excitement inside yourself. You were afraid of saying anything wrong. You were afraid of saying or doing anything that would cause God to remove His presence."[iv]

Without delay opposition arose from the irreligious as well as the religious. There were criticisms regarding denominational ties, the prayer meetings, the services and finances. (Campbell's accounting records to the Faith Mission show the absurdity of such accusations, he lived on very little). He was even condemned for wearing brown shoes rather than the clergy black! Many ministers disagreed with Campbell's doctrine of the baptism of the Holy Spirit and did not want him coming to their area and spreading his "heresies." There were even some who alleged that the devil had sent Campbell to cause division.

One such village where both the believers and non-believers resisted the revival was Arnol, a town of about 400. The first meetings were poorly attended and there was much spiritual opposition. One night after a service 30 gathered to pray, including five church leaders, in the home of Donald and Bella Smith.

"A deacon said to him that night, 'Mr. Campbell, God is hovering over, and He is going to break through.' Yet the meeting was completely ordinary. Still, the deacon was confident and said to Campbell, 'Do not be discouraged. God is coming. Already I hear the rumblings of heaven's chariot wheels.'"[v]

After praying for several hours, Duncan Campbell asked the local blacksmith, John Smith, to pray. He prayed for 30 minutes and ended with this plea, "dear God, there are five ministers in this meeting and I don't know where one of them stands in your presence, not even Mr. Campbell. But if I know anything at all about my poor heart, I think I can say, and I think that you know, that I'm thirsty. I'm thirsty to see the devil defeated in this parish. I'm thirsty to see the community gripped as you gripped Barvas. I'm longing for revival and God you're not doing it. I'm thirsty and you promised to pour water on me. God I now challenge you to fulfill your covenant engagements."

At this, the granite cottage shook, causing dishes to rattle and a pitcher to fall off a sideboard and break. Campbell then related, "I saw a dozen men and women prostrated upon the floor. They lay there speechless as God gave a witness to their hearts. He had taken the field. The forces of darkness were going to be driven back. Sinful men were going to be delivered. We knew something had happened.

"And when we left that cottage at three o'clock in the morning we learned what it was. Everywhere men and women were seeking God. As I walked along the country road, I found three men on their faces, crying to God for mercy. There was a light in every home; no one seemed to be thinking of sleep."[vi]

The effects were astounding, Campbell later pointed out, "I don't believe there was a single house in the village that wasn't shaken by God." The local saloon was closed within 48 hours, never to reopen.

On a trip to Bernera, Lewis; Duncan Campbell reported, "I found the people were very cold and stiff. Calling for some men (from Barvas) to come over and pray, I particularly requested that a

young man named Donald accompany them."
Donald MacPhail had a gift of prayer and Campbell
referred to him as the Evan Roberts[vii] of the
Hebrides. "As we were in the church that night,
Donald was sitting toward the front with tears falling
off his face onto the floor. I knew Donald was in
touch with God in a way that I was not. So I
stopped preaching and asked him to pray. Donald
rose to his feet and prayed, 'I seem to be gazing into
an open door and see the Lamb in the midst of the
throne and the keys of death and hell on his waist.'
Then he stopped and began to sob. After he
composed himself, he lifted his eyes toward heaven,
raised his hands, and said, 'God, there is power
there. Let it loose!' And at that moment the power
of God fell upon the congregation."

"When I said amen," Donald later
recalled, "and looked around me, I was amazed, for
people were on their faces in the pews. Many were
bent over the pews. There were also those who went
into trances or fainted. The power of God was
intense. It was a wonderful evening of the
revelation of God's presence and power.

"That night, and during that time of
divine visitation, a number of people came to
Christ."[viii]

Another small, isolated village did not
look favorably on the reports they received of the
transformation of neighboring towns. Campbell
knew of their resistance and was quite surprised
when Peggy Smith sent an urgent request for him to
come and talk with her about ministering in that
village.

Campbell, accompanied by Pastor

MacKay, came to Peggy's home to discuss with her the wisdom of this leading in view of the fact that Campbell had not received an invitation from the village. Peggy, undaunted by his hesitation, responded with a bold rebuke. Andrew Woolsey writes, "She turned in the direction of his voice, her sightless eyes seemed to penetrate his soul. 'Mr. Campbell, if you were living as near to God as you should be, He would reveal His secrets to you also.'"[ix]

The humbled minister suggested that the three of them spend the morning in prayer. As they prayed on, Peggy confidently reminded God of the conversation they had just hours earlier. "Lord, You remember what You told me this morning, that in this village You are going to save seven men who will become pillars in the church of my fathers. Lord, I have given Your message to Mr. Campbell and it seems he is not prepared to receive it. Oh Lord, give him wisdom, because he badly needs it!"[x]

It was agreed, Campbell would go. He arrived that evening in the village and found a crowded building with many standing outside. It seemed as though the way had been prepared. In his first sermon, Duncan strongly warned them that in "the times of their ignorance God winked, but now commandeth all men everywhere to repent." Of those who deeply mourned over their sin that evening were seven men who became the foundation of the local church in that formally adverse village.

In 1952, a few days before Easter, Hector MacKinnon spent the day praying in his barn on the island of Berneray. God gave this church elder a promise that He would be "as the dew unto Israel" and revival would sweep the island. He was certain God would send Duncan Campbell and prayed "Lord, I don't know where he is, but You know, and with You all things are possible. You send him to the island."[xi]

Many miles away in Bangor, Ireland, Duncan was speaking at a conference when he felt impressed to leave immediately and go to Berneray. Three days later he landed on the island, unannounced and found that a service had been scheduled for that evening.

"The first few services were uninspiring. Duncan felt tired and spiritually out of breath, but the elder adamantly affirmed that revival was at hand.

"One evening as they were preparing to leave the church the old man suddenly took his hat off, pointing excitedly in the direction of the congregation which had just left the service: 'Mr. Campbell, see what's happening! He has come! He has come!' The Spirit of God had fallen upon the people as they moved down towards the main road and in a few minutes they were so gripped with the subduing presence of God that no one could move any further. Amid sighs and groans from sin-burdened souls prayer ascended to God on the hillside. The entire island was shaken into a new awareness of God as many lives were saved and transformed during the following days."[xii]

The revival continued on in what Campbell referred to as waves. The first "Big Revival" was from 1949 to 1952 and several more waves took place after that.   The dates are not completely clear as to when all these occurred, however, the years 1957, 1960 and 1968 seem to surface when researching revival in the Hebrides.

During the second wave of revival, a story is told of two 15 year old girls who were instrumental in bringing revival to their island.   One of the young ladies had visited Barvas, a few years prior, while the Big Revival was going on.   As she told her friend about the amazing things God had done there, the two of them covenanted together to seek God until He "poured water on the thirsty and floods on dry ground."   They met for months on Tuesday and Friday nights for prayer.

One night, one of the young "lassies" saw a vision of Duncan Campbell coming to their island.   The next day she went out to the road to wait for Mr. Campbell to come by.   At this same time in her village, a group of young men had gathered with the local minister to order whiskey for the weekly party they held in the parish hall.   One young man, Angus surprised the group by saying, "I think this time we need to order more than we've ever ordered before because I think we won't be doing this again."   The other young men questioned him as to why he thought this, jokingly asking if he thought the revival they had heard of in other parts would come to their island.

As the young girl stood on the roadside weeping and praying for the many unconverted on her island, she looked up to see Duncan Campbell ride by on a motorbike.   He stopped when he saw her and together they knelt on the side of the road for three hours in prayer for God to visit the island.

Angus was the first to feel the effects as he fell to his knees under great conviction of sin. The others soon followed and even the minister was converted. Revival had come to the island and 15 years later Campbell revisited the island and found that the church was still crowded with many of those converted during that revival.

One remarkable trait of the Hebrides Awakening is that simultaneously, the Spirit of God swept into the churches and then through the villages. One man claimed, "It seemed as if the very air was electrified with the Spirit of God." For days, even weeks, men and women would be under deep conviction before finding relief for their souls. Duncan Campbell even related that there were times he would see men walking the streets, wringing their hands and sobbing, "Oh God, hell is too good for me." The Christians would know who had been converted by their attendance at the daily prayer meetings.

The Hebrides Awakening knew almost nothing of backsliding. Campbell stated that he could count on one hand the number of Christians that stopped attending the prayer meetings, which was how they determined if someone was backslid. An eyewitness commented, "One thing that is characteristic of a genuine revival that is not characteristic of a campaign; very few go back into the world. The work is genuine, lasting."

The fruit of the revival can truly never be known here on earth. Not only were countless souls converted during this time, but also many men and women went into full time service. Some went to foreign lands and a number served as pastors after receiving their training.

      Another lasting effect that could not be measured was that for many, a new place was gained in the school of prayer. Those who came to Christ during this revival learned the secret of persistent, prevailing prayer. In 1968, a minister reported a fresh outpouring of the Holy Spirit, especially among teens. When asked to explain it, he said, "I believe this has broken out because of the steadfastness (in prayer) of the young people who found the Savior during the Big Revival years ago."

Endnotes

----

[i] Colin & Mary Peckham, Sounds from Heaven (Fern, Ross-shire, Scotland, Christian Focus Publications, 2004), 85-86.

[ii] Ibid., 47.

[iii] Andrew A Woolsey, Channel of Revival (Edinburgh, The Faith Mission Publishing Department, 1974), 118.

[iv] Peckham, 220-221.

[v] Michael L. Brown, Holy Fire (Shippensburg, Destiny Image Publishers, 1996), 125-126.

[vi] Ibid., 125-126.

[vii] Evan Roberts, a young man of prayer, was the primary evangelist of the 1904 Welsh Revival.

[viii] Peckham, 236.

[ix] Woolsey, 119-120.

[x] Ibid., 120.

[xi] Ibid., 140.

[xii] Ibid., 141.

Revival is always a revival of holiness.
And it begins with a terrible conviction of sin . . .
Sometimes the experience is crushing. People weep
uncontrollably, and worse! But there
is no such thing as a revival without tears of
conviction and sorrow.
— Brian Edwards

Without a revival, sinners will grow harder and
harder despite preaching.
Your children and your friends will remain unsaved if
there are no revivals to convert them.
It would be better for them if there were no means of
grace, no sanctuary, no Bible, and
no preaching, than to live and die
where there is no revival.
— Charles Finney

Revival in its essence is nothing more than our
finding Jesus again after having long struggled in
other directions for the answer
and at last finding Him—not by some higher
attainment, but by taking the place of sinners again.
— Roy Hession

This is what the LORD says, "In the time of my favor I
will answer you, and . . . will make you to be a
covenant for the people,
to restore the land . . . to say to the captives,
'Come out,' and to those in darkness, 'Be free!'"
Isaiah 49:8,9

chapter two

HEBRIDES TESTIMONIES

As with any revival, this story is actually made up of many stories of the individuals who were convicted, forgiven and transformed. Although they struggled with how to describe this wonderful, terrible Presence, the Hebrides' witnesses have done a commendable job in presenting what cannot be adequately conveyed using human language. Another difficulty they encountered in telling these stories is that often, those who heard their testimonies had no point of reference. "You cannot explain revival to anybody who hasn't been in it" stated one eyewitness. "I don't think there is anything in Christendom today that can compare with revival. No good campaign, no wonderful meeting; there is just no comparison at all. Because in revival, God is completely in control and the whole community is aware of that."

The Youth

As previously stated, the Hebrides Revival greatly affected the young people. In fact, a whole age group was confronted with the reality of the living God and each had to make a decision. One woman, looking back, acknowledged that a "generation was touched. My generation was touched. We were teenagers at the time and the whole teenage world was touched at that time. Many of them rejected and turned away from God but they could never be the same again. Many of them were saved and of course were never the same again."

As with many young people, prior to the revival, they were given over to seeking pleasure rather than God. Social activities many times included alcohol, such as the case with the dances held in the parish halls. However, when "God stepped down," He would invade these dances either converting the whole group or dealing individually with them. One night He sought out a young man who was the M.C. for a dance being held in Carloway on Lewis Island. "I was shattered, I had to leave the dance and go out. I wept my eyes out. I was under absolute conviction of sin. I had met with God. It was a face to face experience with God."

Spread of the Revival

So many were being converted that the places of pleasure were being closed for lack of interest and the young people were flocking to the meetings. "There was no quenching of our desire for the Lord and for the things of God. There was no need to entertain us or put on any special program at the church. We were just hungry for the Word of God itself."

One reason for the spread of the revival was that people could not keep silent about what God was doing. William MacLeod said, "Another result of the revival was the boldness which we all had; boldness to witness, boldness to rejoice, boldness and such freedom to tell to whoever was listening that we had given our lives to Christ. This was part and parcel of the revival. We were so full of [revival] that we could not help but talk about it!"[i]

People were converted every night at the parish halls and during the after-meetings. Campbell "did preach sin and did preach condemnation and he preached hell, but the way of salvation he reserved for the after-meetings, when those who were genuinely seeking God were present. He didn't preach salvation to the unrepentant."

These meetings took place usually during the early morning hours following the regular services. Those who attended "the after-meetings were those who couldn't do anything else; they were absolutely in agony under conviction of sin and of the judgment of God."

The services, after-meetings and prayer meetings went on continuously. In one town, businesses closed daily from noon until 2:00 pm for the afternoon prayer meeting. "It didn't matter what you were doing. You were dying to get to the prayer meeting. You were praying without ceasing, all the time for the meeting, for the people, that they would be converted. The Spirit of the Lord was pouring on you and you didn't know where it was coming from."

No one knew what was going to happen during the services. The length of the meetings didn't matter and "sometimes went right through the night. There were times we were coming home at 6:00 in the morning from such meetings."

Conviction

There was such deep conviction at the services that one man recalling the services as an 11-year-old boy stated, "there was an awareness night after night of God searching me." Another affirmed, "Folks were so much under conviction of sin that they could see no hope whatsoever for themselves. There was a very real work done and a very thorough work done."

Conviction was one of the most apparent characteristics of the revival. "This was no easy believism. There was deep conviction as the solemnity of eternity fell on the people. People wept and were broken over their sins. They knew that they had to stand before Almighty God and give account. Eternity was real; heaven was real. Their plight was terrible, their judgment certain and eternal. How wretched their condition, how unenviable their position before a just and holy God. They knew that they were doomed and damned. Outside of Christ they knew that there was no hope. Truths which they had known and believed in their minds were now living realities as they realized their desperate need of God's mercy and salvation. Campbell's insistence on the true knowledge of sin and of needed repentance from it produced a deep conviction of sin which characterized the movement."[ii]

The spread of the revival caused some of the unconverted to live in dread of their village also being swept away in a divine flood. On the east side of the Island of Lewis a young man actually prayed that God would keep Campbell away from his village. His sister had been to Barvas and brought him news of what God had done there. To his dismay, Campbell did come and after a few nights of resistance the young man finally attended one of the services. God was in zealous pursuit of this soul.

This particular night "the speaker referred to those who had made vows to serve God when in danger at sea but had not fulfilled them. 'That's me!' he said to himself; his boat had been torpedoed during the war. 'My sister must have told him about me. I'll settle with her when I get out!'

"But conviction seized him, and increased the next day when Duncan visited his home and prayed with him. By evening the burden of sin was unbearable and at the service when Duncan asked seekers to meet with him in the vestry for prayer, he was ready to scramble over the crowds to get there!

"Duncan prayed with him and pointed him to the Scriptures but he could not grasp the message of salvation. Despairingly he thought: 'I'm

lost, really lost! There's nothing but hell for me!'
His whole being seemed suspended between heaven
and hell.

      "At last Duncan said: 'I think you had
better pray yourself.'

      "'But I have no prayer,' he objected.

      "'Then just ask the Lord for mercy.'

      "He fell on his knees and uttered only
a few words when the miracle happened. The
intolerable burden slipped away and the joy of
forgiveness flooded in. Looking down he seemed to
see materialized on the floor the locks and chains of
sin which had bound him. He leaped up in an
ecstasy of love to Christ thinking that he was going
straight to heaven. Later as he met an elder by the
roadside, a circle of light seemed to envelop them,
and looking up to locate its source he found himself
gazing into the face of his Savior."[iii]

      A known drunk, Norman Maclean,
had survived an enemy attack during WWII. His
ship was torpedoed and he never forgot the screams
". . . some of them calling for their mothers, they
were friends and they died." He lost 27 mates that
day but the Lord spared his life.

      Maclean was persuaded to hear
Campbell speak one evening but left in a rage
believing someone to have betrayed his corrupt
behaviors to the minister. The next day he sought
to drink away the memory of the service but it was
too late, he had "caught the *curam*" (Gaelic for deep
conviction). The following day was worse. "Paddy,"
as he was called by friends and family, was terrified
to meet Christ in his wicked state and knew that
God would be just in damning him to hell forever.

He had to get to another service but now Campbell was on the other side of the island. The man traveled across the island, attended the meeting and returned home at 2:00 AM. Immediately he went out back to his shed, fell on his face in brokenness and asked Christ do with him as He pleased.

Norman later became a Church of Scotland missionary. He was never a polished speaker but his sermons were bold and saturated with the fire of heaven.

Those that were converted before ever entering a church also confessed to the same feeling of terrible conviction, few could escape it. People who had not been in any of the meetings would come to see Duncan Campbell at the church during the day claiming that they too had been touched by God. He would ask why they came to see him or what touched them? Often the reply was, "It's what's here [in the church] just now. It seems to be in the air. It doesn't matter where I go, I can't help thinking of the things going on."

When assurance finally came, the joy was all the more complete. A woman converted without anyone praying with her knew she had passed from death into life. In quoting Isaiah 53, she testified, "with His stripes you are healed and I felt healed. I knew I was healed. Nobody had spoken to me, but God had spoken. No person had pointed me the way but God had pointed the way and I knew I had passed from death unto life, from the power of Satan unto the power of God."

The deep conviction of sin was not confined to the unconverted. Even the Christians were constantly confronted with the reality that this

God who visited the Hebrides is a Holy God. A man warned, "Those people who say, 'Oh that we had revival!' I don't think they know what they're asking for because it can be a terrible thing when you're face to face with God. It's what I've found in my own personal experience. You're up against something completely not of this world, it is supernatural. The awareness of the holiness of God is something that really is difficult for anyone to describe."

Sensitivity

Christians also experienced another invaluable effect of God drawing near; an obvious rise in their spiritual sensitivity. "Have you done business with God today?" was a frequent greeting by the roadside. Christians were instinctively drawn to homes where others were praying, or where someone was seeking the Lord. It was not unusual for people to immediately stop what they were doing when moved by God – for instance one woman while milking a cow felt she must immediately stop and go plead with a neighbor to yield to Christ.

Another remarkable story involved the new convert, Norman Maclean (Paddy). One night he had a dream that a black bird was knocking at the window and he knew this was the Lord showing Him that someone was soon going to die. Shortly after this dream, Paddy was asked to drive a busload of 29 youth to Ness lighthouse for a holiday outing. He agreed with the stipulation that he would be given permission to bring his Bible and speak to the youth regarding their souls. While stopping to picnic along the way, he ministered to the young people about the Savior and pled with them to see their need of salvation. Norman knew that one of them, Bobby, was that soul who would soon face eternity. Later that day, while playing football at Ness lighthouse, Bobby fell over a cliff and died the next day.

"As the revival continued, no one was more sensitive to the movings of the Spirit than Duncan himself. A minister with whom he stayed, related that he often knew beforehand who was going to be saved. One day, looking across a loch to a house on the other side, he remarked to his companion: 'Donald, there's a young woman who is going to find the Savior in that house tonight.' It happened exactly as he said."[iv]

Manifestations

Many historic revivals have reported manifestations of the Spirit in the midst of the move. The Hebrides was no exception. Christians had dreams even before the revival began in which God told them He was coming. One man in a dream saw an angel passing over villages, indicating to him which ones God would be visiting.

There were many reports of "faintings and trances." Kenny Ban told of scenes he witnessed, "On some occasions some fell into a trance for the duration of the meeting. They would not be a disturbance at all but would sit silently with hands upraised. When they came around at the end of the meeting, their words seemed to have the scent of heaven. We were awed at times and at other times they simply left the meeting with us all, having met with God personally in this unusual way."[v]

Alexander MacLeod, who was one of the Barvas praying men, said, "The first time I ever fainted in a meeting was on one occasion when I was last to pray. As I prayed, I was suddenly made aware of the state of the lost in our district. A great burden fell upon me as I interceded on their behalf. Eternity seemed to open up to my view and I felt my strength leaving me. I simply passed out. The intensity of that burden has left me but I have never forgotten those moments."[vi]

Prayer

One characteristic reported over and over again by the Hebrides Christians was the amount and intensity of prayer, before and during the revival. Prayer to them was not something to be done if your schedule allowed, it took first place in their lives. They understood the power and price of true intercession.

Colin and Mary Peckham write, "All that which we deem to be so very necessary for success, in God's eyes, may not be so necessary after all. In fact these issues might well get in the way of better things. They could well be hindrances and not the necessities which we thought them to be. We can be so occupied with the trappings when God is waiting for the worship and adoration of our hearts, He is waiting for us to get to the place where He can put within us something of the burden which He bears for a lost humanity, which will then in turn drive us to our knees to intercede mightily in the power of the Holy Spirit. . . . There is a cross at the heart of true intercessory prayer, a burden, a passion, an agony. "[vii]

The prayer of one elder brings to light the overwhelming influence intercession had on the young people. "The prayers we heard on that night will always be indelibly written on our minds. I can still picture the elder with uplifted hands and tears coursing down his cheeks supplicating the Throne on behalf of us young people – travailing in soul as he described us 'on the slippery paths of darkness.' His petitions were as the arrows of the Almighty in our souls. What a privilege to have been there!"[viii]

Obviously intercession did not diminish once the revival came, in fact it increased. Jack MacArthur recalled the necessity of prayer during the revival. "There were men there who recognized that although God had come and revival had come, it didn't absolve them from further prayer. It placed them under a burden to pray more. When Duncan Campbell had a hard time and was to have another meeting, some men went home. They knew that they had a mission to fulfill, and so when Duncan was preaching they were at the house praying through, broken before God – supporting!"[ix]

Changed Lives

Mary Peckham (Morrison)

Mary Morrison grew up with a knowledge of God, her unsaved family even held daily devotions. She knew the Bible because Scripture memorization was a mandatory part of her public school education. Yet at eighteen, she was living on her own in Glasgow with no interest in God and no intention of returning home to Lewis to live in the constant shadow of religion.

God, not willing that Mary should perish, brought her back home to have an encounter with Him. "Revival was the talk of the place" Mary related. "Go where you would, they would be talking about what had happened the night before, or the night before that, when so-and-so had come to the Lord. 'Did you hear, Mr. X who has been such a drunkard, is now praying in the prayer meetings?' And so it would go on."[x]

At first Mary was very resistant to the Spirit's moving however she eventually gave in and began attending the services.

"Every night I walked to the church to hear the preacher thunder forth the judgments of God. He stormed up and down the pulpit, expounding Scripture and preaching damnation to the lost and salvation to those who repented and savingly believed. I knew one thing – this man was sincere. He preached on an eternity without God, on the power of the Cross, on the glory of the redeemed, on the wonders of heaven. Oh, the gospel rang forth. It was terrible in the ears of sinners but thrilling to those who had responded and yielded to the Savior. It was no easy believism."[xi]

Mary's conversion was long and difficult as she went from resistance to despair to desperation and finally prayed through until she obtained salvation. Those who come in this way do not soon turn back and Mary was no exception.

As was typical with those saved in the revival, Mary and her friends couldn't get enough of church and prayer meetings. They would go from meeting to meeting all night not arriving home until early morning. She humorously tells a story about one late night going with her friends to a meeting they thought would be taking place in Barvas. Upon arriving, they found that there was no meeting so they promptly went to the parsonage and woke Pastor MacKay telling him they were looking for a meeting. Campbell, who was staying there, forfeited the few hours of sleep permitted him that night to get up and minister to this hungry group of young people!

A call to the ministry came to Mary soon after her conversion yet she was reluctant to accept it. There were many reasons she felt it could not be the call of God. Women preachers were not accepted in the Hebrides, she felt wholly inadequate and, hardest of all, her parents (now converted) would never approve of her going into the Faith Mission.

Through a series of confirmations, including Campbell confronting her once about her call, Mary was finally convinced that God had a work for her to do. The opposition was great but she completed her training and was sent out with another woman to hold missions in various places in Scotland. God used this team in wonderful ways to bring the message of the cross to those who might otherwise have never heard.

In 1957, Mary along with three other female mission workers, were sent to an island in the group of Hebrides called North Uist. As they prayed night and day, God began to grip the hearts of the people in several villages. Conversions became a normal occurrence so they sent for Duncan Campbell to come and assist with the work. Mary writes, "The movement probably reached its height at Tigharry when, in that very rural setting, the first meeting began with 111 people full of expectancy. Kate-Ann Shirran remembers the power of the singing in the meetings. 'Revival singing is anointed singing,' she said. 'It is like a fire that goes through one's whole being.'

"Eventually the papers got hold of the story. On 12th February 1958, a report in the Daily Record announced, 'Girl Preachers Rock an Island.' Sales at the local bar plummeted and the Sunday Express came to get the story of all that was happening during those remarkable days."[xii]

Mary continued to serve the Lord in any area opened to her, even traveling as far as Canada and South Africa. It was during one trip to South Africa in 1969 that she was joined in marriage and ministry to Colin Peckham. They continued to serve there for the next 14 years, 12 of which were at a Bible college in Cape Town. Eventually Colin accepted the position of principal at the Faith Mission Bible College, where they served until retirement. The Peckham's final years were busy with writing and itinerate ministry. Both are now home with Jesus, leaving this world only months apart. (As the author, I am very grateful to both Colin and Mary for their generous help in reviewing this book and setting the record straight on some of the errors and inconsistencies I encountered in researching the Hebrides' stories.)

Fay Hay

A high school student named Fay enjoyed attending dances and concerts with her friends. One of her friends, Chirsty Ann, had a lovely singing voice and often sang at the concerts.

One day Chirsty Ann told Fay that she was feeling increasingly anxious about her soul and felt she should give up performing at the concerts. Fay, thinking that her friend had become fanatical, was determined to continue attending her social events and yet she was beginning to realize that all the entertainments were, in the end, utterly worthless.

Just before Christmas of 1949, she received the news that Chirsty Ann was converted the night before. "I was thunderstruck, not having a clue what had happened to her. So I went down to see her. There she was, and I just took one look at her and she was transformed. There's no other word for her face, glowing! So I said, 'you've got it.' She said, 'oh Fay, we were so blind. It's not *it* at all; it's *Him* – the Lord Jesus Christ.'"

Chirsty Ann's conversion was the turning point for Fay. She could not escape the knowledge that she was far from God and wanted what her friend had. A few days later, Fay attended a service with Chirsty Ann.

"The time came for the meeting and we went into the church. The church was absolutely packed. Right away, the singing of those Gaelic Psalms gripped my mind and set open unto me the gifts of righteousness. I sat there and sobbed and sobbed quietly, tears running unto the floor. Duncan Campbell preached beautifully out of the

Song of Solomon; 'The voice of my beloved, the one that is showing Himself through the lattice.' He talked about the hindrances, walls that separate us from God. I knew all about that, but I didn't know what they were, I only knew they existed. He said, 'you're sitting there saying but I do pray,' and I was just at that moment thinking, 'but I do pray.' And he said, 'but what do you pray for?' And I thought, 'I'm asking God to make me good.' He said, 'you're asking God to make you good. My dear friends, if God could make you good why did the Lord Jesus Christ have to come into the world? What a prayer. God cannot answer it.' I thought, 'oh, I am undone.' The only prayer I had he said was a blasphemy and I realized it was. Really for that moment, I believed I was totally without hope.

"After having been shown that I could never have had my prayer answered because it was impossible, he said what was possible, the Lord Jesus did. He came to bridge this terrible gulf, to demolish this terrible darkness, to bring us back to God. And it was just as Song of Solomon went on to say that like the singing of birds, is the heart freed from this awful, awful darkness. The Lord Jesus Christ actually setting one free and [I] sat there marveling how on earth [I] could never understand it when [at that moment, I] knew it all so well. It was actually happening. [I was] from that moment a child of God through the Lord Jesus Christ."

At least one other service had a profound effect on Fay. While singing a hymn one evening, she was given a glimpse of hell and the terror of eternal judgment. In response to this vision, she prepared herself for the mission field.

While in college she met her husband, John Hay, and together they served as missionaries to Thailand. Eventually they returned to the Hebrides and it was there that Fay heard one final time the "voice of her Beloved" calling her home.

Donald MacPhail

Previously covered was the account of a young man called upon to pray at a service in Bernera. Donald MacPhail, a 16 year old prayer warrior, also has a story worth telling.

The presence of God was not something you could escape from, for even out in the fields of the family croft (farm), questions about God and eternity relentlessly plagued Donald's mind. At one point he recalls envying the sheep he tended because they were not tormented as he was.

Donald was converted in the spring of 1950 at a house meeting in Arnol. "After the cottage meeting I endeavored to leave for home, but on looking around outside the house, I noticed a man praying by the side of the wall. Shouts and heavy sighs were heard from the people within, as if crying for help. I could not restrain myself any longer and touched that godly man. In a broken voice I told him that I wanted to get right with God before it was too late. As he turned I saw Christ in the very expression on his face. In compassion he took me by the hand and led me into the prayer meeting."[xiii]

Campbell was dependent on the '39 revival intercessors and recruited them as well as new converts to assist in prayer for the meetings. Donald was privileged to be one of those who would pray through for the services shortly after his conversion. Campbell usually called for them to begin praying at 4:00 PM in the church or building where the services were to be held until the meeting began. In this way, Donald later commented, he learned how to do ministry from Campbell's example.

Donald received a call to the ministry through a message preached by Campbell about a year after his conversion. He first fulfilled his compulsory two years of military service then returned to Arnol to help out at home. He continued to put off Bible College until an unexpected visitor appeared at his door.

"I owe much to the discipling of Duncan Campbell, for I was much on his heart. He sensed that things were not going well with me spiritually and he made the laborious journey from Edinburgh to come and see me in Arnol. He confronted me with my failure to enter the Lord's service and my apparent unwillingness to do so.

"He said, 'The Lord has sent me from Edinburgh to come and speak to you because you are being disobedient to the heavenly vision. You are avoiding the vision and the call that God has given you. You are not obeying His voice."[xiv]

Donald struggled with the call for another month but finally found peace when he wrote a letter of application to the Bible Training Institute in Glasgow. After completing Bible College and language studies, Donald left in 1962 to serve as a missionary in Yemen. He married in 1965 and he and his wife, Christine continued to work in the Middle East for over 40 years.

Ruined for Anything Less

Undoubtedly, no one who experienced this historic outpouring could ever forget what God had done. As one woman bore witness, "You've been brought into touch with the power of the world to come and something, something indefinable lives with you. You can never be content with anything less than with what you have seen and you live to see it again."

Endnotes

----

[i] Peckham, 108.
[ii] Ibid., 88.
[iii] Woolsey, 122-123.
[iv] Ibid., 123.
[v] Peckham, 105.
[vi] Ibid., 161.
[vii] Ibid., 126.
[viii] Ibid., 174.
[ix] Ibid., 86-87.
[x] Ibid., 139.
[xi] Ibid., 140.
[xii] Ibid., 157.
[xiii] Ibid., 234.
[xiv] Ibid., 238.

Saturate me with the oil of the Spirit
that I may be aflame . . . Father, take my life, yea, my
blood if Thou wilt, and consume it with
Thine enveloping fire. I would not save it, for it is not
mine to save. Have it, Lord have it all. . . .
Pour out my life as an oblation for the world. . .
Make me Thy fuel, Flame of God!
— Jim Elliot

The man with a cross no longer controls his destiny;
he lost control when he picked up his cross.
That cross immediately became to him an
all-absorbing interest, an overwhelming
interference.
— A.W. Tozer

Following hard after Jesus forces us to make daily
choices to pursue Him rather than the things of
earth. The person desiring a life of radical pursuit
must narrow his interests. As the thought "earth has
nothing I desire" consumes our heart, the clutter
demanding our time and attention is treated as a
thief attempting to steal our most valuable treasure.
— Glenn Meldrum

"I looked for a man among them who would build up
the wall and stand before me in the
gap on behalf of the land"
Ezekiel 22:30

chapter three

CAMPBELL'S TESTIMONY

Duncan Campbell asserted that there were three outstanding experiences in his life; salvation, baptism of the Holy Spirit and a life-altering confrontation with God. He referred many times to these events in his preaching and each are worth relating in order to understand the man.

Conversion and Holy Spirit Baptism

Campbell was born in 1898 in the Gaelic speaking area of northern Scotland; hence, he was termed a "Highlander." His parents were Christians, having been converted through the efforts of the local Faith Mission when Campbell was a small child.

As a teenager, Campbell did not embrace his parent's faith. The major obstacle for him was his love of concerts and dances. He was a piper (bagpipe player and dancer) and was in the spotlight on many of these occasions. However, he had praying parents.

One night during a performance, Campbell related he was "frightfully disturbed in my soul" while playing. He said to the chairman, "I've just made this discovery that I'm on my way to hell." The chairman, who was also a minister, said not to worry, it would pass. Wisely, Campbell did not wait for it to pass but left the concert. On the way home, at 11:00 PM, he went by the Faith Mission in which a prayer meeting was still going on. As he passed by, he heard a familiar voice praying, it was his father praying for the community and his family. Campbell went in and sat next to father but soon left under deep conviction. "I felt I would fall into hell." At 2:00 AM he arrived at the farm and went into the barn to meet alone with God.

"God I know not how to come," he cried, "I know not what to do. I know not how to come. But my God, I'm coming now. Oh, have mercy on me." At that moment, "God swept into my life. I was born again. It was real. It was supernatural."

Campbell joined the armed forces during WWI. He came in as a soldier of the Highland Brigade but was soon transferred to the Cavalry when it was discovered he was an experienced horseman. Looking back on this time of his life, he confessed that even though God "kept me from open sin, the inbred sin was troubling me, keeping me in bondages. The heart is deceitful above all things." It was here that God met with him a second time.

In 1917 Campbell was severely wounded at Passchendaele Ridge in Belgium, one of the bloodiest campaigns of the war. As he went down, his horse rolled over on him, injuring his spine. He was convinced that he was dying, blood was everywhere and his dead horse lay beside him. The Scripture came to his mind "without holiness, no man shall see God." The dying soldier felt utterly unworthy to meet God.

The Canadian Cavalry was also called out to assist in the battle. As they were charging, one of the horse's hooves struck Campbell. The man hearing Campbell groan came back after the charge to rescue him. The young Canadian put him on the back of his horse to transport him to the nearest casualty clearing station.

Campbell surveyed the many lying dead on the field and wondered why he had been spared. He recalled a prayer of Robert Murray M'Cheyne's: "God make me as holy as a saved sinner can be." This became his all-consuming cry to God. It was then that the Spirit met him and he knew he was "baptized with the Holy Ghost."

As proof of his Spirit baptism, he relates that in just a short time at the Station, seven Canadians were converted as he prayed the Psalms aloud. A very miraculous work without a doubt, yet an even greater wonder considering that he prayed in Gaelic, knowing little English at that time in his life. This he considered his "first experience of revival power."

Campbell was taken to a hospital in Scotland to recover and there for seven months he saw God working. "Just by sharing a word about Jesus, people were saved." At his release, his parents suggested that he go to seminary, but he felt it a waste of time to take five to seven years to prepare for ministry when "in a matter of minutes, God could save."   Instead, he attended the Faith Mission's nine month training school where young people could be equipped for mission work at home and overseas.

Early Ministry

The Edinburgh school was run by John George Govan, whose lectures were "no dry as dust sessions for acquiring theological facts" but were full of life and power. Mr. Govan believed that even more than education, the students needed encounters with God. At times, lectures were forgotten, as God moved in and they all went on their knees and remained in prayer for hours. He "recognized that such meetings with God would accomplish more to equip these lives for service than lectures could ever do."[i]

Upon completion of his final term, Campbell was disappointed to learn he was assigned to Ireland rather than the Highlands for which he longed. Yet he obeyed, went out with fellow workers and in spite of strong opposition, established a solid mission in Ballybogey. Unexpectedly, Duncan received a letter asking him to travel immediately to Scotland and begin a work in the district of Argyllshire.

During these years God was awakening the British Isles often through the work and prayers of "pilgrims" sent out by the Faith Mission. At this time in their history there were almost 90 workers, Campbell being one of these that witnessed the power of God transforming villages.

For five years the young evangelist traveled with a Faith Mission worker from Ireland, George Dunlop. From town to town they went and "God swept in just talking about the Savior." One of the most well-known outpourings took place in 1921 and was spoken of for years throughout the British Isles. Campbell testified that he "saw the hand of God in revival because of the fuller work of grace experienced on the back of a horse."

A visitor to one of the missions in Argyllshire testified, "Up to 200 were packed into the schoolroom. They came to listen with interest and sincerity. Conviction of sin began to be felt and the cry, 'What must I do to be saved?' came from penitent souls. Boys and girls in their teens, as well as men and women, up to and over seventy years, were seeking the Savior. Even people unable to attend the meetings were deeply concerned for their souls."[ii]

One woman was asked if she would be going back to the dance halls now that she was a believer. She promptly pointed out that there were no more dances since all the dance hall promoters had been converted and now spent their evenings at church or prayer meetings.

In the town of Kinlochleven lived a young woman who was very hard to the gospel. She was finally won through the preaching of Campbell and Dunlop. When asked why she had finally given in, she replied that these men where different from other preachers she had heard all her life. She sensed that the two mission workers were truly concerned for her soul so she had to respond to their pleadings.

In 1924 Campbell was sent to the Isle of Skye to begin new mission works. He met with much resistance in the first town, especially from the religious community so he took to walking the roads at night, pleading with God to rend the heavens. There were three young women of prayer living in that village who were also interceding for their community.

One evening following a disappointing service, Campbell spent the night praying in a barn. The three women also spent the night in prayer in a cottage. After midnight one of the women had an assurance that God at last had come and He was going to work but they must continue to pray through until the morning.

"[The] next night the power of God fell upon the meeting. Souls groaned under the convicting power of the Spirit of God. One woman left the meeting crying: 'I'm lost! There's no mercy for me!' She was brought back in and fell to the floor. No one could help her until God revealed the saving power of His Son and brought peace to her troubled soul.

"Attendance increased. The presence of God was felt through the entire community. Whole families were brought to Christ. . . . The old postman was a terrible drinker. No one thought of inviting him to the meetings. Probably he would not have gone if he had been invited. But one night he was so peeved that he had been overlooked, he thought: 'I'll go just to spite them'.   Off he went. God took hold of him and soon he was rejoicing in Christ."[iii]

It is at this point in the telling of his life's story that Campbell reminds us that you can "never get to a place where it's impossible to fall."

For five years Campbell served under the Faith Mission and had learned much about praying in his needs.   The organization did not pay the workers, they were to go out by faith and believe God for their daily food and shelter.   There were times when Duncan's faith was greatly tested in this.

In July of 1925 he left the Faith Mission to come under a formal, recognized denomination because he had long desired to marry Shona Gray, a Highland woman.   Campbell felt he could not adequately provide for a family unless he took this step which would secure for him a regular income.   They were married in December of that same year in Glasgow.

Divine Confrontation

The first church the couple pastored was a United Free Church in Ardvasar.   They were there from 1925 until 1930 when Campbell was appointed to shepherd a flock in Balintore until 1940.   His last pastorate was in Falkirk, a financially prosperous city in the industrial south.   Each church brought greater battles and the final church seemed to drain him of life.   "When you work with iron, the iron gets into your soul," he later confessed.

"For 17 years," Campbell recounts, "I moved in a barren wilderness.   It was true that I was evangelical in my preaching, so much so, that on several occasions I was asked to address the Keswick conventions because I was the 'candle of the '21 Revival.' I was Campbell of the Argyllshire Revival. God in His mercy gave me a measure of His mercy. [Yet], 17 years of knowing in my heart I wasn't right with God . . . feeling out of touch. On my knees before God, again and again I acknowledged Him until one morning [He confronted me].

"I was preparing for a Keswick Convention. In my study at 5:00 AM I heard someone singing; my daughter, Sheena. Something about her singing gripped me." Though only 16 at this time, Sheena enjoyed a deep relationship with her Savior and had already accepted the call to go to Nepal as a missionary.

She came into the study, put her arms around her father's neck and asked to have a talk with him.

"Sheena, I would be happy indeed to have a talk with you, but first of all, might I ask you what it is that is moving you this morning?"

"Oh Daddy, isn't Jesus wonderful! Isn't Jesus wonderful!?"

"Sheena, what is it that makes Jesus so wonderful to you at 5:00 this morning?"

"Daddy, I've just spent an hour with Him. For several days, I've been battling against facing you with this question, but I must do it. When you were a young pilgrim, before you went in for the ministry, you saw revival. How is it Daddy that you're not seeing revival now? You have a large congregation and many are joining the church, but Daddy, when did you last kneel beside a poor sinner and lead him to Jesus?"

Campbell declared, "That shook me. I vowed to God that if He didn't bring me back to that experience that I had on that horse's back, I would give up the ministry. My dear people I meant it! I would be anything but a deceiver. I went to my study to have a session with God. I cried to God to forgive me. In about one hour, God had come to me to bring me back to the fullness of blessing of the Holy Ghost. I lay there with this power coming over me I could not explain.

"I had a vision of hell. I could see multitudes, multitudes, streaming over the caverns of death to be doomed and damned eternally. What a vision, oh, what a vision. At that moment the door of the study opened and that dear lassie came in and lay down beside me. And I can almost hear her voice now as she prayed to God saying, 'Oh Jesus, keep his reason.' She was afraid I was [having a breakdown] because of the vision. Suddenly it left me, but left me weak. A voice seemed to say to me, 'Go back to the Faith Mission, give up the ministry. You've suffered much by what you've listened to in the church for 17 years. You've been in a barren wilderness. God has come to you again, obey God.'

"At that moment the old question rose again. The children (five of them) are not yet educated. They will have to face college, is that possible in the Faith Mission? For a second or two darkness came into my soul, darkness came into my mind. I was facing the cost of this decision, when suddenly this angel of God spoke. 'Daddy, Daddy, whatever it costs go through with God. I believe you are facing the question that if you go back to the Faith Mission, because I am fully persuaded that God is asking you to go back, perhaps you're wondering how you can look after us. I know that you've promised to give me a new coat on my birthday, but Mommy will be quite willing to change my old coat. I don't need a new coat.' It was that that did it. She was willing. Thank God, I said yes to God. God said go out and tell it again.

"I wrote three letters resigning my charge but kept my position as a Presbyterian minister. I was free to go out. In a very short time, I found myself in the midst of this revival (Hebrides) that continued for three years and has kept coming wave after wave."

Faith Mission Reports

In their book, *Sounds from Heaven,* the Peckhams dedicated two chapters to extracts from Faith Mission reports made by Duncan Campbell during the revival. The following selected entries taken from their book give an abbreviated sense of the wonder and excitement of living in such times.

Barvas, Lewis; December 1949

"We are in the midst of glorious revival. God in His great mercy has been pleased to visit us with showers of blessing, and the desert is rejoicing and blossoming as the rose. Some of us will live to praise God for what our ears are hearing and our eyes are seeing these days in Lewis... Meetings are crowed . . . continue until 3:00 and 4:00 o'clock in the morning . . . we are dealing with anxious souls in every meeting.[iv]

Isle of Lewis, January & February 1950

"Revival fires are spreading, and at present it looks as though other parts of Lewis are coming under its sway.

"Meetings have been larger than ever; hundreds have been crowded in, and many turned away. I may say, I am now at it night and day, and just getting sleep when I can. The largest meetings are now in the parish of Ness.

"Meetings continue to be crowded and souls are being saved every day, with some outstanding cases. In my last report I mentioned two pipers being saved, who were to have been at a concert and dance that night. A minister from the district where the dance was held, and who was in the meeting, felt led of God to go home and visit the dance and tell what had happened. He did so, arriving there at 3 o'clock in the morning. After some opposition from the leader he was allowed in; he there and then gave out Psalm 50, the last three verses. God's Spirit fell upon the gathering and in less than ten minutes men and women were crying for mercy. The first to be saved was the leader of the concert party."[v]

Carloway, Ness, Arnol; March & April 1950

"I addressed five meetings today. We simply cannot get the people away and meetings will continue until tomorrow morning. Revival has gripped much of the island.

"We are in the midst of the greatest move yet. The Spirit of God is mightily at work, and many have come to the Savior. I am writing this report in the early hours of the morning, having dealt with the last lot of anxious ones at 1:30 AM . . . God is mightily at work. So great is their conviction of sin, that strong men have even fainted behind their looms (for making Harris Tweed).

"I began my mission here in Arnol in the midst of the most bitter opposition. Opposition meetings are being held about 200 yards from the church in which I hold my meetings.

"We are in the midst of a glorious revival here. Opposition has vanished, and the whole district is moved. People are being saved at work, and in shops work is being suspended, churches are crowded, and crowds outside. People were coming to the meeting last night bringing their own chairs to sit on outside. So deep the distress of many, that we had to remain helping them until morning." [vi]

Leverburgh, Harris; June 1950

"This has been a week of hard fighting, but I believe victory is in sight. I have been up against strong opposition from the usual source, but my eyes are toward God, and already the enemy is yielding. My great difficulty is accommodation, as the church is too small for the crowds that are coming. . . . This has been a very blessed week. The real break came on Thursday, and since then we have been in the midst of a very blessed move of the Spirit. Men and women have yielded to Christ in every meeting . . . I look back with gratitude to God for all I have witnessed of the mighty power of God during the past six months." [vii]

Isle of Lewis, November 1950

"As I sit down to write this report the words of Psalm 107 come to mind, 'Oh that men would praise the Lord for His goodness.' We are in the midst of revival, and what scenes! The whole district is stirred. I counted eight buses taking the people to church today, not to mention cars and vans – crowded meetings and men and women finding the Savior. . . . Men who never went to church, and who were regarded as hopeless, have been gloriously saved. In one community all the young men are saved or in deep distress of soul. I shall value prayer for guidance. I am being pressed to return to this district, but other places are waiting for me to fulfill my promise to them."[viii]

Ness & Kinloch, Lewis; January & February 1951

"There was a mighty manifestation of the power of God in the meetings last night. Wave after wave of Holy Ghost power swept over the meetings and strong men were broken down and crying for mercy. . . . People have been in such distress that they have cried out for mercy in the services others fainted."[ix]

Baile-Na-Cille & Uig, Lewis; October & November 1951

"People walk miles through wind and rain, and will wait through three services between 7:30 and 3:00 in the morning. . . . Our meetings this week were characterized by physical prostrations and swooning, and the agony of godless men whose consciences awoke was terrible to see. Men have been found walking the roads at night in distress of soul; others have been found during the day praying among the rocks."[x]

Isle of Lewis, January 1952

"Last night we witnessed a mighty manifestation of the power of God. As a young lad from Arnol was praying, God swept in, in power, and in a few minutes some people were prostrated on the floor, others with hands raised up fell back in a trance. We were in the midst of it until 1:00 o'clock in the morning."[xi]

Later Years

Duncan Campbell continued his itinerant ministry for several years throughout the British Isles and beyond. Place after place where he visited, "God's presence accompanied him in an unusual way. God seemed to give him an extra dose of the supernatural, demonstrated not so much in powerful and amazing works, but in people becoming aware of the presence of Jesus, the glory of the Lord, and the nearness of the heavenly world."[xii]

In 1958 Campbell was offered the position of principal of Faith Mission Bible College in Edinburgh, which he accepted, however he continued to minister at churches as much as possible. Many students were affected through his preaching and example. One student recalled, "There was something sacred about the way he used God's name, and often the atmosphere of heaven filled the room when, with reverence and tenderness, he simply said, 'Jesus.' We felt we were standing on holy ground."[xiii]

Every Friday morning was spent in prayer and waiting on God. It was during one of these meetings that God visited the college on March 4, 1960. "A deep sense of God filled the place when the Principal spoke from Habakkuk 2:1: 'I will stand upon my watch, and set me upon the tower, and will watch to see what he will say unto me, and what I shall answer when I am reproved.'

"Then as a student began to pray for revival in his own life the power of God fell upon the group. Some wept silently; others cried out for cleansing. One girl said: 'I never knew what the fear of God was until then; it seemed that if I lifted my head I would look upon God. I never knew what sin was until then; outside the grace of God I felt fit for hell.'"[xiv]

After the first wave of the Hebrides Awakening, Campbell had started an annual convention in Stornoway on Lewis Island. He looked forward to being reunited with the converts and was introduced to new ones each year. Before returning to the school, he would visit the beloved praying men of Barvas on the other side of the island.

"He marveled at their discernment and world-wide vision in this far northwestern island. Calling to see one of them he arrived at the house to hear him in the barn praying for Greece. He could not understand what interest a butcher in Lewis could have in Greece.

"'How did you come to be praying for Greece today?' he asked him later. 'Do you know where Greece is?'

"'No, Mr. Campbell, but God knows, and He told me this morning to pray for Greece!'"[xv]

After his retirement from the college in 1966, Campbell kept a rigorous schedule of itinerate preaching. He had been yearning to do this since he first put in his resignation in 1963 (it had taken three years to appoint a successor). Although constantly battling sickness, he accepted many invitations to preach throughout the world.

His messages were often a plea to the church to repent from their sin and compromise; to turn from their shallow faith saturated with materialism. He often pointed out that what "the world needs to see is the wonder and beauty of God-possessed personalities; men and women with the life of God pulsating within, who practice the presence of God and consequently make it easy for others to believe in God."[xvi]

One farmer while returning home after hearing a challenging sermon remarked to his friends who traveled with him, "You never hear Campbell preach without going home to pray."

While in the States, Campbell was introduced to Loren Cunningham, founder of Youth With A Mission. Cunningham was praying about opening a School of Evangelism in Europe where students could be taught by visiting ministers. A building was soon purchased in Switzerland and another center was established at a later date in Greece. Campbell became one of the best loved teachers at both locations, his lectures always linking evangelism and revival.

"Successive sessions of students came

under the spell of the Highland prophet in Switzerland, and also in Greece, where he ministered to a group in the beautiful fishing village of Porto-Rafti. The outstanding feature of his ministry was the unique way in which he reproduced himself in the lives of these young people. Several young, married couples who came under his influence in Greece later became leaders of a spiritual advance in Europe.

"Here is a student's personal reminiscence of one of his sermons:

"Prior to Mr. Campbell's coming we thought we had arrived! Then conviction came, real conviction. Small things we thought were harmless became sins in our sight."[xvii]

One might be tempted to think that Campbell lived the rest of his life basking in the memory of what he once experienced. However, he stated many times that he was always pursuing more of God and would never be content to live with past recollections when God could surpass anything he had yet witnessed. "Live in the memory of it! Never! We must live for greater things! No victory is secure except by greater victories!"[xviii]

Duncan Campbell never retired from God's calling and ministered right up to the end. He often battled illness and had to be hospitalized at times. Mary Peckham recalled once in 1957 that she felt a heavy burden for Campbell and spent most of the day in prayer for him. She later learned that while ministering in Pretoria, South Africa, he suffered a severe hemorrhage and had to be rushed to the hospital.

On March 28, 1972, Duncan quietly

departed from this world to be with his beloved Savior. In his last sermon, preached just four days before his death, he reminded a group of students of the cost of discipleship.

"The New Testament reveals Jesus as a realist. He will never be popular; His followers need never expect to be. He will have men follow Him knowing the cost . . . it means a fight! Keep on fighting, but see that you are fighting in the love of Jesus!"[xix]

Endnotes
----

[i] Woolsey, 58.
[ii] Ibid., 68.
[iii] Ibid., 72-73.
[iv] Peckham, 47-48.
[v] Ibid., 48-49.
[vi] Ibid., 50-51.
[vii] Ibid., 53.
[viii] Ibid., 55.
[ix] Ibid., 57-58.
[x] Ibid., 61.
[xi] Ibid., 63.
[xii] Wesley Duewel, Revival Fire (Grand Rapids, Zondervan Publishing House, 1995), 315.
[xiii] Ibid., 316.
[xiv] Woolsey, 172-173.
[xv] Ibid., 161.
[xvi] Ibid., 177.
[xvii] Ibid., 185.
[xviii] Ibid., 189.
[xix] Ibid., 190-191.

Life-giving preaching costs the preacher much –
death to self, crucifixion
to the world, the travail of his own soul.
Only crucified preaching can give life. Crucified
preaching can only come from a crucified man.
— E.M. Bounds

We are not diplomates but prophets,
and our message is not a compromise
but an ultimatum.
— A. W. Tozer

The man whose little sermon is "repent" sets himself
against his age, and will for the time being be
battered mercilessly by the age whose moral tone he
challenges. There is but one end for such a man—
"off with his head!" You had better
not try to preach repentance until you have pledged
your head to heaven.
— Joseph Parker

The true prophet of God is not concerned first of all
about the nation or even about the Church. He is
concerned that God is insulted openly.
— Leonard Ravenhill

For though I preach the gospel, I have nothing to
glory of: for necessity is laid upon me; yea, woe is
unto me, if I preach not the gospel!
1 Corinthians 9:16

chapter four

CAMPBELL'S HEART

Duncan Campbell's sermons and writings contain repeated truths that are encouraging as well as very convicting. He was a bold, fiery preacher holding the untiring attention of his hearers as he warned of God's judgment and His abundant mercy. "There was nothing complicated about Duncan's preaching. It was fearless and uncompromising. It was prophetic preaching, not diplomatic, and the hearers were called to make a clear choice, for there was no middle path. During the revival the wrath of God was emphasized and coming judgment. God had given him this emphasis."[i]

"A minister described [Campbell's] preaching as 'kill-joy stuff', but interesting enough, the young folk whose joys he was supposed to be killing, were those who appreciated most the ring of reality and challenge to godly, sacrificial living which he presented. Scores of young lives were transformed and dedicated to the service of God."[ii]

Evident and interwoven in his messages are the deeper life teachings of holiness, brokenness and compassion toward the lost. The following quotes and comments, compiled from several of his sermons, are grouped together by subject rather than by actual messages.

Revival Characteristics

One observer stated of the Hebrides: "Real revival is when truly, things of the earth take complete second place and only the Lord and His kingdom seem to count." This definition of revival is a fact of every holy visitation. Another truth Campbell asserted was: "In revival, God steps down and His presence fills the community and perhaps in a matter of hours, scores are brought to Jesus Christ."

"It is God's work, for God's glory." He related often to the powerful conviction and the willingness of the people to let God do the work even to the point of leaving a soul in distress, terrified by their sin, that the Lord might bring them to true salvation. His belief was that Christians need to let people "stew in their conviction. Leave them there, let God deal with them. We take things out of the hand of God by our counseling. We [must] get to the place where we leave [the] work to Him."

"In the northwest of Scotland, if you were to press yourselves, your advice, and your help upon an anxious soul, you'd be inclined to believe that it was man's work, just man's work. And [a sinner] would much rather be left so that God Himself would handle it. That is why we've known people for weeks and longer, in distress of soul before light broke in upon them. But you go back to those villages today; you haven't a single backslider in most communities. When God does a work, He does it well."

"Revival doesn't begin among sinners," Campbell points out, concerning the Christian's responsibility, "it begins among people dedicated to a purpose. God is the God of revival but we are the human agents, which make it possible. I know that revival belongs to God and in that field God is sovereign. But let me say that I do not believe in any conception of sovereignty that nullifies man's responsibility.

"Are you in the place where God can trust you with revival? Are you one He can use, are you one He can trust? Nothing can possibly happen unless God comes down. The state of things brings you to this.

"[We are in a] state of lawlessness (referring to Isa. 63:19), an utter disregard for God. The prophet [Isaiah] presents a powerful argument for revival." To promote this truth, Campbell quoted Charles Finney as saying: "The low condition of the church is a fitting argument for confidence and belief in the God of revival to do something about it."

The main characteristics of the Hebrides Awakening (and should be of any revival), according to Campbell were; the fear of God, great conviction of sin, importance placed on the Scriptures, very little backsliding and large numbers called into ministry. It is also important to note that two of the things that do not matter in revival are time and programs. "In revival, time does not exist . . . the presence of God puts to flight programs. Often, I've cried to God: 'So move in our midst that the program will go and the presence take the place.'"

In his book, The Price and Power of Revival, Campbell addresses the criticisms concerning emotional responses often displayed in the services. "We are afraid of disturbing people today. 'You must not have their emotions stirred, you must not have people weeping in a meeting, you must not have people rolling on the floor under conviction of sin; keep things orderly.' May God help us, may God have mercy upon us. Who are we to dictate to Almighty God as to how He is going to work?"[iii]

Man's Efforts And Easy Believism

Campbell often makes a comparison between man's efforts at evangelism and God's work in revival. He is very adamant in his opinion that evangelistic meetings should never be referred to as revival meetings. Revival "is a moving of God in the community and suddenly the community becoming God conscious before a word is said by any man representing any special effort.

"We praise God for evangelistic campaigns and special efforts, but as a general rule, these do not touch the community. It remains more or less the same and the masses go past us to hell! You cannot substitute anything for the God of revival.

"We have seen man's best endeavors in the field of evangelism leaving the community untouched. We've seen crowded churches, we have seen many professions, we have hundreds, yes thousands responding to what you speak of here [in the U.S.] as the altar call. But, I want to say this dear people and I say it without fear of contradiction, that you can have all that without God. Crowded churches, deep interest in church activity is possible on mere human levels.

"Perhaps I should say here, personally I am tired of this trafficking in decisions. This gospel of [easy] believism has cursed your country and mine. God deliver us from easy believism! Did Christ make it easy? I did not find my own conversion easy. When a man has come to the end of himself, he has reached the beginning of God.

"I would make bold to say that this in itself, is one of the supreme causes why revival tarries in America; this gospel of simply believism. A lazy Christianity that is unwilling to recognize the supernatural or face the implications of Calvary. You know as well as I do, the great cry in America and in Great Britain is preach a positive gospel. The positive gospel is, invite men and women to believe in Jesus Christ. I want to say this evening; there is a negative side as well as a positive side to the gospel — that is repentance. 'Let the wicked forsake his way and the unrighteous man his thoughts and let him return unto the Lord, and He will have mercy upon him' (Isa. 55:7). For every time Jesus spoke about heaven, 13 times he spoke about hell.

"I don't believe that one single soul can be saved until he's prepared to recognize the lordship of Christ over his life. That means self-denial; that means following Christ, obeying Christ. It means separating from the world, turning to Jesus with full purpose of heart to serve Him. You mean to tell me a person can be saved who is not prepared to do that. No more than the devil."

To illustrate the church's declining view of the lordship of Christ, Campbell referred to a recent conversation he had with a missionary serving in the Congo. "Since that awful massacre in the Congo we've only had two missionaries offering for service and the two of them are women." Campbell noted, "I believe that the reason for the slowness and unwillingness of young men to offer themselves for Christian service today is just because there is no lordship of Christ over their lives. They didn't recognize [this] when they made their decision and consequently, Jesus is not the center of their lives.

"I've been told, 'you're too narrow.' But the way is narrow. Andrew Murray said, 'It is comparatively easy to win people to a cross, but to a cross that leaves them uncrucified. Oh, beware of the cross that leaves you uncrucified.'

"The doctrine of [easy] believism . . . it's sending multitudes to hell." In warning ministers, Campbell emphasizes, "I dare not compromise in order to accommodate the world, the flesh or the devil. But see the tendency today is to do that. I want to say dear people, tolerance at the expense of conviction and righteousness is just playing into the hands of the enemy. Once a man is commissioned by God, he must go through with God though every voice in the world is crying out 'come down, change your methods.'

"My dear people in this field compromise is the [curse] of the Christian church today. There seems to me to be a gradual coming down so you hear words such as accommodate and tolerance. 'Accommodate, oh we must try and accommodate them. And in order to capture the [worldly], we must become sort of [worldly].' Oh God help us!

Holiness And Fear of God

Campbell was often asked why it is that revival has not come with all the prayers, conferences, etc., to which he frequently quoted Isa. 59:2, "But your iniquities have separated you from your God" (NIV). He expounded, "I would say that sin in the Christian church . . . is the basic reason why we're not seeing revival, there is sin in the camp. Calvary will not cover what you've got to uncover."

Secret sin, Campbell believed, is one of the main hindrances to revival. "There is no small sin in the sight of God. I must be willing to get into the light. Once in the light, I must willingly obey. I can no longer live under a self-created illusion. Honest men will ask God to search them. In the light, you see yourself as God sees you. The nearer we get to God, the more we will discover about ourselves that we never suspected before. Revival begins with personal revival.

"We talk about holiness but are we

holy? We talk about power of the precious blood of Jesus, but my dear people, are we clean? Perhaps you are professing holiness. It's easy to make a profession, but oh give me the mark, give me the evidence. And the evidence is New Testament holiness. That cries aloud separation. That speaks of passion and burden and a cry for revival."

In relation to the link between holiness and revival, Campbell remarked, "I think again of those people in the Hebrides. How they longed and how they prayed and how they waited and how they cried, 'Oh God, rend the heavens and come down,' and all the time God was handling them; all the time God was dealing with them and the process of cleansing went on until the moment came when angels and archangels looking over the battlements of glory cried, 'God, the vessels are clean, the miracle can happen now.' I believe that with all my soul that they are ever gazing over the battlements of glory and waiting for a prepared people."[iv]

Pastor Mackay also understood the crucial place of holiness in revival. "That night when God swept into a prayer meeting and revival began, I made this profound discovery: the God sent revival must ever be related to holiness."

In one sermon Campbell used a quote from Robert Murray M'Cheyne that stated, "What a man is on his knees before God is all that he is, this and nothing else." Campbell continued, "What I am is far more eloquent, far more convincing than anything I could say. What a man is on his knees may be very different than what he is in the pulpit. If I am so different in the church to what I am in the home, help me [God] to acknowledge it. I believe the world expects something different from us. Character is what you are in the presence of God. Reputation is what you are in the presence of men.

"What we need today is the baptism of the fear of God. These are the days when we feel little and hear little of the fear of God. Oh, let the fear of God grip us. Let the fear of God cause us to tremble. Let the fear of God so come upon us that sin would become something terrible, damnable and devilish."

Campbell believed that there were no short cuts to the move of God. He knew there was no substitution for holiness. In using a Samuel Rutherford quote, he brings to light the usefulness of a man who is holy, "A holy man is a terrible instrument in the hands of God."

Humility, Brokenness and the Cost

There was no question as to the importance Duncan Campbell placed on humility and brokenness. These attributes were apparent in his life in the way he continually gave glory to God for all that was accomplished though him. Often when speaking about revival he stressed the fact that he did not bring revival to the Hebrides, but that others prepared the way. He also spoke very openly of his own failings and his need for God to break him. In relation to revival, humility and brokenness are not side issues.

"If the answer is revival why is revival not coming? . . . There must be a great number of people today . . . men and women who are burdened and are longing for revival. They recognize that revival is the answer. Why then is revival not coming? Has God ceased to be interested in the souls of men? Is He quite happy to see them drifting to hell to be doomed and damned forever? Oh, that is not the God we believe in. But I think about that verse of Scripture, it seems to me we have the answer in it: 2 Chr. 7:14. If revival is the only answer, in a sense we've got the key to it in our hands. 'If my people called by my name will humble themselves and pray' . . . God is not obliged to send revival because we pray, but He is bound by covenant promise. He is to send revival when we humble ourselves and pray. Brokenness of spirit. Put your pride in your pocket!

"We need vision and I believe vision comes when we're in the process of breaking. Evan Roberts prayed and prayed, 'Oh God bend us, oh God bend us.' He meant Oh God break us. The place of brokenness is the place of transformations."

Campbell used the account of Jacob in Gen 32 as an example of brokenness and God conquering the self-life. "There came a moment when God conquered him. Jacob received a mark of identification [a limp] after being confronted with God, now he could only cling.

"Our supreme need is for God to come. Man in the final analysis, can do nothing but throw himself on the sovereign mercy of God."

In trying to correct the myths concerning revival, Campbell repeatedly spoke of the sacrifice and cost of it. "The altar speaks of sacrifice and every visitation of God costs in human lives." John, chapter 12 tells of some Greeks making a request to meet Jesus saying, "We would see Jesus." "Today we say, 'oh, we would see revival.' But you can't find where they did see Jesus. Between asking to see Him and Jesus hiding Himself, He speaks on the grain of wheat that dies . . . I hear in that statement that we're presented with a challenge; are you prepared to die? Are you prepared to face the implications of Calvary? Dead to the world.

"Jesus knew what was in man; He knew all that was in the heart of the Greeks. And He knew that they weren't prepared. I believe Jesus saw and Jesus knew that they would not face the implications of Calvary when confronted with them. And He quoted the truth; 'Unless a grain of wheat falls into the ground, it abideth alone, but if it dies, it bears much fruit.' And then He went and hid Himself. I make bold to say that they never saw Him. 'If any man will come after me, let him deny himself, and take up his cross, and follow me (Mat. 16:24).'

"When did the fire fall [on the altar] (1 Kings 18)? When the altar was built and the last piece of [the bull] was placed on the altar. That last piece of meat to my mind is just an absolute surrender to the will of God, whatever that may mean. Is there a fire burning on your altar tonight? For 17 years as a Presbyterian minister, my altar was broken.

"For God to act, the last piece of the bull had to be put on the altar. You have consecrated again and again, but your consecration was too often mingled with defective elements of self-preservation. You can talk and pray about revival until doomsday and your prayer and your consecration will be just the laughing stock of devils. It's the last piece of [the sacrifice], God demands all."

Prayer and the Word

In every genuine move of God prayer is what brings it and prayer sustains it. In the Hebrides, there were more people attending the prayer meetings during this visitation than attended church before the revival.

It is also interesting to note that prayer was considered the expected result of a valid conversion. One witness commented that you could always tell who had been converted the night before by who was at the daily prayer meeting (held from noon to 2:00 pm). In fact, you were not considered a Christian until you regularly attended the prayer meeting. "When a soul is born again," noted Campbell, "suddenly, there is created a hunger to be among the praying people of God. The prayer meetings become crowded."

A minister who saw God sweep his parish understood that prayerlessness is a great hindrance and that many who say they want revival are not willing to pay the price in prayer. He said, "When I was over at Kinlock with Duncan Campbell before there was any indication that there was a spiritual movement in the area, he mentioned that we should send for reinforcements and he meant praying people. In most communities, you find people who will enjoy the fruits of revival but are not prepared to pay the price of being burdened. As a minister of the gospel, I would emphasize the necessity of prayer . . . He uses human instruments."

Campbell agrees, "We think about an awakening and we talk about the need to do something definite for God, but somehow little is being done. Well you have evidence of that of what you see in the prayer meeting. I could bring you to a church in London where on a Sabbath you may see anything between two and three thousand listening to the preacher. But if you go to the Wednesday prayer meeting, you're fortunate to get 30. Tell me; is Sunday morning or Sunday evening the indication as to the spirituality of that congregation? No, what you'll see in the prayer meeting on Wednesday indicates the depth of spirituality."

Much of the blame of the church's spiritual condition Campbell attributed to the value the clergy often placed on work over prayer. "The devil is not greatly concerned about you and work, oh no. You can work and work and work again and he doesn't mind that so long as he can keep you from God."

The "morning watch" for Duncan was the most vital and protected part of his day. He understood the necessity to be alone with God or he would have nothing to give. "The prayer life must be fought for," he insisted; "everything will militate against it. The world with its pressures and speed will give us no time; the flesh with its appetites and weaknesses will rob us of concentration; Satan will concentrate his subtle powers to contend every inch of the prayer-route. The tide of battle turns in the closet; this is where the real warfare is accomplished. It is there Satan is served with an authoritative notice to quit."[v]

The importance of the Word of God was also stressed by Duncan Campbell. He advised that the Scriptures be a vital part of daily family devotions. In the churches, he believed Christians should be "taught from a theologically conservative view."

In North Scotland, the word of God was freely taught and preached. Even the unconverted knew the Bible. It is interesting to note that Southern Scotland, which experienced no visitation, was suffering from the heresies liberal seminary professors were promoting. When questioned about this by a professor, Campbell declared, "Here in the South you ministers and you professors have robbed the people of the authority and inspiration of the word of God with your damnable philosophy and theology."

Souls

Concern for souls was effectively modeled in the life of Duncan Campbell and he believed this to be the norm for everyone who calls themselves a Christian. "I have very little faith in the Christian profession of any person that hasn't a burden to save souls, to lead souls to Christ a minute or two after he is conscience of the fact that God saved him. Yes, the man who professes salvation and who hasn't a burden to pray for souls ought to question his own experience; was he ever born again?

"Tell me dear people, do we recognize our responsibility? Do I realize my responsibility in the face of the desperate situation that confronts me today? In the face of the appalling state of the Christian church and the masses careless to their doom? Tell me; is there any sense of responsibility? God needs watchmen. God cries for laborers. God sees that soul that you could influence. But you disobey and that influence may pass that soul and pass that soul forever. My dear people, God needs you. God needs you."

Campbell used a story of an event that took place during WWI to illustrate the desperation that should be in every heart to save souls. During an attack at Passchendaele Ridge, "I saw on my right a young 42nd Highlander. He was wounded in his arm and trying to tear the tail of his shirt to bind it. Another soldier in front of us lay wounded beckoning for help. I heard that 42nd Highlander say, 'I'm sure that's Jock!' I saw him spring to his feet that wounded arm lying beside him as he climbed saying, 'yes, that's poor Jock and I'll save him or die in the attempt.' My dear people, how often I've thought of that. Oh, for that spirit! 'I'll save them or die in the attempt.' Around us today there's bruised, bleeding and broken humanity drifting to hell. But how many of us have that spirit of the 42nd Highlander? In the natural life we live to die, but in the spiritual life, we die to live. How few of us are prepared for that?"

Holy Spirit, Obedience & Anointing

One reason Campbell faced opposition from the Christian world was due to his constant reference to the Holy Spirit. He believed in a second work of grace, which he claimed to have experienced for himself, sometimes referring to it as sanctification or consecration, but most often using the term the "baptism of the Holy Ghost." He believed "a Pentecostal experience is gloriously possible today. I would say that if Pentecost cannot be repeated then we are living in a period in world history when the word of God has neither pattern nor precedent. If Pentecost is the living link between the eternal purposes of God and the world that must inevitably perish, truly our supreme need is a Pentecostal visitation."

Campbell allowed no one an excuse for not receiving this baptism. "The God that did it for me can do it for you. I believe in a covenant keeping God. What has all this to do with you? Perhaps you're in a congregation, perhaps in a community that needs God. Brother, are you prepared to recognize that the answer is the Baptism of the Holy Ghost?" This was not a side issue to Campbell, he clearly believed that unless we give the Holy Spirit His correct place in our midst; we will not see our community changed, we will not see revival.

Another issue that came out when Campbell would address leaders was the sin of preaching without the Holy Spirit's anointing. "Preaching truth without the anointing of the Holy Ghost" he alleged, "is helping the devil to damn souls. Oh my dear people, it's true, there is nothing on earth today so deadening as preaching without heaven's anointing. I dread the thought that I should ever stand before a congregation without heaven's anointing."

In one sermon, Campbell tells a disturbing story of a Puritan that had a vision of the devil preaching the gospel on a street corner. He asked Satan why he would preach the gospel? "Because I have made this discovery, my best weapon for the damning of souls is to get men to preach the gospel without anointing."

Campbell related, "I used to say to my students in Edinburgh, be careful in dealing with souls that you're under heaven's anointing. In case in your endeavor to counsel a seeker, you're helping the devil to damn him."

One more important note in regards to this subject that must be included is Campbell's solution to securing an anointing that will be of divine usefulness. It does not come from education, books, or from implementing the newest church growth principals. He knew the secret and practiced it. He would not minister, unless "my address [was] steeped in prayer. Oh brother ministers, how much time do you give to waiting upon God? How much time do you give in the morning to the morning watch? 'My soul wait thou only upon God, for my expectation is from Him.'"

The other factor in having heaven's anointing or obtaining His blessing is obedience. Duncan put the will of God above man's wishes and at times was severely criticized or misunderstood. "[Is] God in control of your life? We must ever regard obedience as a fundamental condition for blessing; a truth that must never be disregarded. I want you to clearly understand that obedience predisposes an unreserved yielding to the claims of Jesus Christ."

An interesting facet of the Hebrides Awakening in relation to obedience is the natural response of the Christians and new converts to making restitution if possible. There were testimonies of long time debts paid with interest, stolen items returned and relationships healed. One man even went to the U.S. for a year to earn enough money in order to pay back all those he had stolen from.

Opposition & No Compromise

In revival the enemy wages war against the saints; more so than at other times. As Campbell puts it, "you're not going out to a picnic, you're going out to a battle, you're going out to face an enemy that is out to defy God and defy every known Christian principal. The devil is here to frustrate the purposes of God. In every engagement with the enemy, it is deeds, not words or much activity that measures the value of my life. In other words, it's how you react to the challenge that you face."

Speaking to church leaders in North America, he used a verse from Isa. 59, which declares, "Truth is fallen in the streets" (Isa. 59:14). "My dear people," he warns, "it seems to me it's [fallen] in the streets in your country today. In spite of all your crusades, in spite of all your decisions, truth; vital, dynamic, saving truth, regenerating truth has fallen in the streets and the devil is trampling triumphantly over it.

"Brother, I believe the time has come when men and women of similar convictions must stand together for [these] truths: holiness, godliness of living, separation, purity of action, purity of being, purity of conduct.   We need that today because truth is fallen in the streets."

Quoting the next verse, "He who departs from evil makes himself a prey," Campbell revealed another source of opposition.   "The man who will take his stand for righteousness, for truth, for holiness, for Holy Ghost separation . . . the man who takes his stand for that truth will not be popular today I can assure you.

"[The] man of God, Nehemiah, was called upon to do a great work, rebuild the walls (of Jerusalem).   And that work he did; but not without opposition.   There were those there that were against him.   They wanted him to come away, to lower his standard.   [He responded], 'Should a man such as I flee?'   They were doing their utmost to get him to leave the wall, doing their very best to get him to come down.   In other words, to lower his standards to worldly conformity.   But should 'a man like me run away?' or as we have it in our Gaelic Bible, 'Will a man like me run from it?'   You see, he was a man that fought through because he was convinced he was called and chosen.

"Here we have a man who obeyed God and obeyed God rather than man.   God had commissioned him and God had called him and in spite of all opposition, in spite of misrepresentation and misunderstanding, he went on quietly and definitely and with purpose to fulfill God's commissions.   And he built the wall.   As men and women who love the Savior, who have been called and commissioned by God to be faith builders in the world, we dare not run from the opposition, nor must we ever succumb to it."

"Elijah challenged the powers of darkness. In the name of his God, he challenges [the prophets of Baal] to a test, which would prove whether Jehovah or Baal was supreme. And that is the challenge that you must present in this our day and generation and cry: "The God that answereth by fire, that's my God!

"The answer then, the answer is God. Nothing short of a manifestation of [the] supernatural will meet the dire situation in our land; yours and mine today. Oh, young folk listen; get to know your God. They that know their God shall be strong. The God of Elijah is alive!"

FINAL ADMONITION

In this day of spiritual famine in our land can we hope to see anything like the Hebrides Awakening?   Perhaps if he were here, Duncan Campbell would challenge us as he did others with these disturbing words: "I want to say this, and I say it on the authority of this Book, yes, God will [bring revival] again when He finds a church He can trust; when He finds a man whom he can trust with revival. God found men in Lewis – I have no hesitation in saying that – men whom He could trust."[vi]

"I believe that when God finds the clean hands and the pure hearts we shall see springs in the desert and rivers in the dry places. . . . My dear people, let us get on our faces before God and pray that He may yet visit us in mercy and that we, His people, may once again ascend the hill of God and stand in His holy place. May God grant it."[vii]

If My people who are called by My name
will humble themselves, and pray and seek My face,
and turn from their wicked ways,
then I will hear from heaven,
and will forgive their sin and heal their land.
2 Chronicles 7:14

Endnotes

----

[i] Ibid., 127-128.
[ii] Ibid., 163.
[iii] Duncan Campbell, The Price and Power of Revival, (Fort Washington, PA, Christian Literature Crusade, n.d.), 49.
[iv] Ibid., 29.
[v] Woolsey, 156.
[vi] Campbell, 65.
[vii] Ibid., 69.

Bibliography

Books:

Brown, Michael L., *Holy Fire*. Shippensburg, PA: Destiny Image Publishers, 1996

Campbell, Duncan, *The Price and Power of Revival*. Fort Washington, PA: Christian Literature Crusade, n.d.

Duewel, Westley, *Revival Fire*. Grand Rapids: Zondervan Publishing House, 1995

Peckham, Colin & Mary, *Sounds from Heaven*. Fern, Ross-shire, Scotland: Christian Focus Publications, 2004

Woolsey, Andrew A., *Channel of Revival*. Faith Mission Publishing Department, 1974

Sermon Tapes:

Action and Obedience
And the Country was Filled with Water
Building the Walls
Duncan Campbell: His Testimony and Conversion
Fire of God
God's Answer to the Cry of Unbelief
Heart Preparation for a God Sent Revival
Heart Preparation for Revival
Is the Lord Among Us?
Lewis: Land of Revival
Reality of the Divine in Christian Experience
Revival in the Scottish Hebrides
Revive Us Again
Sacrifice that is Pleasing to God
Sin in the Camp
Then the Fire of the Lord Fell
When God Stepped Down from Heaven

TheRadical**TRUTH**
Podcast

IN HIS PRESENCE MINISTRIES PODCAST
WITH GLENN MELDRUM

TheRadical**TRUTH**

*restoring truth
in a compromised culture*

a weekly podcast with host,
Glenn Meldrum

Find us:

ihpministry.com
iTunes
Google Play Music

teach the way of God in truth Mk 12:14
In His Presence Ministries

In His Presence Ministries is the husband and wife team of Glenn and Jessica Meldrum. Glenn is ordained with the Assemblies of God and holds an MA in theology and church history from Ashland Theological Seminary. He has ministered as an evangelist since 1997 and pastored 16 years. Glenn, who was saved out of a life of drugs and alcohol, ministers at churches, conferences and recovery programs. Jessica Meldrum is the other half of In His Presence Ministries. She is a Biblical counselor who ministers to women through teaching groups and individual counseling.

The Meldrums are available for church services, evangelistic meetings, conferences and men and women groups.

Please feel free to contact us at: ihpministry.com

Other resources available from
In His Presence Ministries

The Radical Jesus is a brief examination of Christ's life, teaching, death and resurrection. Everything about Jesus is absolutely radical; the One the Scriptures reveal as anything

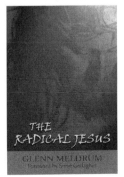

but tame. Without a clear understanding of who Jesus is, we can never hope to be the disciples we were meant to be in this fallen world. The twofold purpose of this book is to exalt the radical Jesus by presenting a fresh glimpse of who He is and to reveal the high calling that true believers are to live.

"If you find yourself drifting into the soul-numbing lethargy of our day, this book is for you."

Rend the Heavens was written to stir spiritually hungry saints to the dire need for a revival in our land. Genuine revival is an invasion from heaven which brings to men a conscious awareness of God. It changes churches and transforms society. This is what it means for the Lord to Rend the Heavens. The greatest spiritual advances the Church has ever made were accomplished through the outpouring of the Holy Spirit. The God of revival has transformed cities and nations in the past. We do not need a new message, but a new anointing!

This book does not lay out plans, programs or strategies, but deals with the issues of the heart as they relate to revival. It was designed to help believers draw closer to Jesus through deep repentance and intimate fellowship, for this is where revival springs forth.

Rescue Me! is a candid investigation into how our character affects every portion of our lives. The unrefined and unconquered portions of our character cause us more harm than a host of adversaries, be they men or demons. From pulpit to pew the church is suffering from a lack of personal and corporate holiness. Our lifestyles of compromise are holding back the tangible power of the Holy Spirit. Once these hindrances are removed the church will become a radical agent of change in a perishing world.

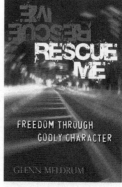

Rescue Me! will help believers understand how the sinful nature corrupts our character and offer biblical answers that will enable us to live the victorious life. This life changing resource includes questions at the end of each chapter making it ideal for personal or group Bible study.

To order books, CD teaching sets or more copies of Floods on Dry Ground, contact: In His Presence Ministries: www.ihpministry.com

The Meldrum's books are also available on Kindle.

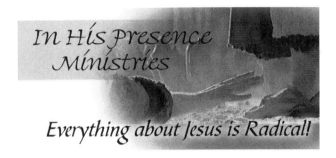

Visit ihpministry.com for additional ways to stir your faith –

- 2-4 minute videos to present the radical essence of the Christian faith

- The Radical Truth Podcast

- Sermons

- Articles

- Teaching videos

Printed in Great Britain
by Amazon

85615646R00054